I0450113

SEX...
"THE SEDUCTIVE ADDICTION"

Sanford Ashley

Edited by Michelle Boone

Bloomington, IN 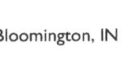  Milton Keynes, UK

AuthorHouse™
1663 Liberty Drive, Suite 200
Bloomington, IN 47403
www.authorhouse.com
Phone: 1-800-839-8640

AuthorHouse™ UK Ltd.
500 Avebury Boulevard
Central Milton Keynes, MK9 2BE
www.authorhouse.co.uk
Phone: 08001974150

This book is a work of non-fiction. Unless otherwise noted, the author and the publisher make no explicit guarantees as to the accuracy of the information contained in this book and in some cases, names of people and places have been altered to protect their privacy.

First published by AuthorHouse 6/22/2006

ISBN: 1-4208-9576-1 (sc)

Printed in the United States of America
Bloomington, Indiana

This book is printed on acid-free paper.

This book is dedicated to the true loves of my life…..

My lovely wife Mona…… "The Mountain Slayer"

My strong son Malachi….. "The Prophet"

My bold son Brandon….. "The Determined One"

TABLE OF CONTENTS

Chapter One: Addicted? Not Me!! 1

Chapter Two: The Root 15

Chapter Three: Boundaries (Protecting the Fortress)..... 31

Chapter Four: Accountability (True Confessions) 49

Chapter Five: Prepare for Good Works 57

Conclusion 63

Acknowledgements... 65

CHAPTER ONE
Addicted?…..Not Me!!

Addicted. A very strong term. Most of us hear this word and immediately think of drugs and alcohol. We would never think of sex as an addiction. The media and society as a whole have glamorized sex in every form and fashion possible. Sex is used to sell cars, clothing, food, sporting events, chewing gum, and even toothpaste to name a few. Cosmetics, vacations and books (oops, no pun intended) use sex to sell products. But seriously, sex was designed for our pleasure in its proper context. God has designed it for a sacred act between man and woman. Now I know that there are some who will read this and they do not believe in God. I will tell all of you this: if a man (or woman) does not understand that sexual promiscuity can lead down to a road of addiction, you are truly misled. You are totally oblivious to the dangers. I know this first hand very well.

My addiction started when I was in college. I would visit go-go bars, and eventually massage parlors two to three times per week. One year I spent an excess of $45,000 on sexual addiction. I used every dime I had and credit cards to feed my addiction to sex. I never graduated to prostitution because I was stopped in my tracks when a prostitute refused to "date" me one evening. Let me tell you this: when a prostitute refuses you, you know that there is a grand purpose to your life! I have been free from sexual addiction since December 1997. Thank God.

I truly believe that I am somewhat qualified to speak on this subject. Sexual addiction is a huge problem with men throughout the world. Many men in business, politics, athletics and entertainment fall prey to this monster on a daily basis. Sex is sold with great seduction. It feels good, looks good, and will enhance your personality, appearance, finances, etc. This is according to society. We are told subliminally that we are defined by how sexy we are. Society sells us the "benefits" of sex, but we are never told about the cost or repercussions of these "benefits". We never count the cost. It is a massive, expensive, dangerous road that one will fall into if not careful. Sex is the subtle sell. Families are devastated by a husband that is caught in the web of sexual addiction. Dreams die in this cesspool of lust. Addictions are formed and birthed from the various choices we make. Addictive behavior and actions are derived from the need for personal gratification. Those that are in the grasp of sexual promiscuity end up worshipping sex. They treat sex as an idol. Pornography, phone sex, prostitution, internet video porn and beastiality are forms of sexual addiction. Rape and molestation are also derived from sexual addiction. Most pedophiles at some point were sexually abused in their life. If these behaviors are not dealt with, catastrophic consequences can possibly occur in one's life. Jealous husbands or boyfriends attempt to harm those who have committed adultery with their spouses and girlfriends. Women are devastated by their loved ones who can't stop looking at porn videos. Some become sex offenders. Exposure to pornography and other graphic material may have happened by discovering pornographic magazines in the home. Maybe it was in dad's private den downstairs. You were trying to find your baseball mitt and accidentally knocked over a stack of magazines. You picked them up and then you saw why dad never came upstairs to read to you at night.

Maybe an older woman at school or the nurse at the doctor's office touched you in a place on your body that made you feel "funny" or uncomfortable. The feelings of shame and guilt were suppressed for years and never dealt with. It forced you to withdraw from women, and you found the company of a man non-threatening. If damaged emotions are not addressed, children and adults will develop an aggression that will fester and grow. There will come a boiling point where the victims of sexual abuse begin to act out on their aggressions and acts that were bestowed upon them. These afflictions can turn a victim into a sex addict. This behavior can lead to rape, molestation and other sex crimes (or crime in general).

Think about this for a moment. My addiction lasted well over 10 years. That is a long time. It started with a simple visit to a local go-go bar. I lost a lot in 10 years, but God gave me back everything I lost with interest. I asked God to forgive me, help me, and He did. Immediate change took place.

Men(and women for that matter),my heartfelt desire is to see that your life will be changed and impacted by my experience with the evil monster of sexual addiction. This book is designed to help each and every one of you step into your destiny and dreams. We will look at some of the "triggers" that allow men to fall into sexual temptation. Most of all we will see how to get out and stay out of sexual addiction. This book is designed to reach anyone with a true desire to be free from this bondage.

Every man has a big gift box that awaits him. Think of it as a trophy. There are many things that you have been trying to obtain, and you just can't figure out why you have not attained them yet! That box is full of businesses, marriages, finances, great health, etc. One thing you will learn from me is that I like to get down to business. I love seeing people, particularly men, advancing in all areas of their lives. I will tell you this from one man to another: if you are caught in adultery, pornography, prostitution, etc., your gift box remains closed. Shut. Sealed with a bow. I can say this because I experienced everything from marrying a wonderful woman, two great sons, a new job with four un-sought promotions, to writing for a couple of national magazines. All of these opportunities were there waiting for me all the time, right in my big fat gift box. I had delayed the opening of my own gift. Why? I was caught up in sexual addiction. Now there are some of you reading this and saying "Hey Sanford. I live a very comfortable life. I've got my custom built home, my golf club membership, multi-million dollar businesses, etc. I don't want to be free from this, I like it." Guess what? Do you realize there are more blessings that await you? Here is a free nugget for you...NEVER THINK THAT YOU HAVE ARRIVED. When you think you have it all, you have just limited yourself, your future, and your opportunities. Don't let sexual addiction limit you as well. Let's look at some key factors in the fight for sexual integrity as well as some of the issues that can fuel this behavior.

"THE TOUGH TEST"

Sex is the toughest area in a man's life to master or put under his submission. Men tend to become under the submission of sex. This is a challenge for men. Men thrive on challenges. We are wired with a warrior's spirit and heart. We love to engage in any type of battle; from playing video games and winning over friends to landing the great contract for the company. Men constantly jockey for position in their careers, finances, and of course, in the lives of women. Society has drilled it into the heads of men that the more women you sleep with and date, the more of a man you are. The media loves this because by using women as a "sexual lure", a man can be sold cars, houses, tickets to games, credit cards, etc. The "residual effect" sex has is enormous. A

5

man can easily develop a spending habit, get into debt, or worse, become a sexual offender. Sexual promiscuity and addiction does not sit still…..it grows.

I saw this happen in my own life and the lives of others. When I was a sales rep straight out of college, I worked with a man we will call Pete. He was the regional sales manager at one of the top office equipment companies in the world. Pete was a man that modeled everything that I thought was great about a man. He had a successful marriage, lived in a great neighborhood, and was wonderful. I would stay late after hours at the office to glean from his life experiences; personal and professional.

I left the company after one and a half years and lost contact with Pete. Two to three years had passed before I ended up seeing Pete again. It was a Friday night and I was out with a few friends and to my surprise I saw Pete. I immediately went over to the bar where he was sitting. When I refreshed his memory and told him who I was, he looked at me with such shame and guilt. You see, Pete AND I were in a go-go bar, looking at women who were very scantily dressed. I talked with Pete for about an hour. I learned that he was no longer married and had been divorced for awhile. He had since lost his job as well. The Pete that I had admired was lost.(Guess what….so was I). He confessed that he had gotten caught up in the "fast life". Money and women flooded his life so quickly that he never got a chance to guard himself against the dangers of sexual addiction. Pete poured a ton of money into liquid lunches at go-go bars. He started to see women outside of his marriage. What started as a small pleasure mushroomed until he became a bona fide victim. A victim of sexual addiction. I could not condemn Pete; I do not have the authority to do so. The true reason that I could not condemn him is that I WAS HEADED DOWN THE SAME DESTRUCTIVE PATH. Here I am sitting in a go-go bar with Pete…caught up in the same small pleasures.

See Pete missed it. Pete always passed the "tough tests" at life. His marriage passed all tests possible for a prosperous marriage. Pete was well balanced with work and home. Pete passed the tough tests at work. He was tough on his sales reps, tough with his peers, tough on his competition. The problem Pete had was where and when he NEEDED to be tough, he wasn't. When he needed to fight, he did not. He was not prepared for the leverage that the money machine gave him to spend where and when he wanted to. Pete traveled with no supervision from the company. He traveled alone and had no constructive plan for how to spend his downtime. His downtime was not planned with any type of purpose. Pete was an accident waiting to happen.

I missed as well. This was a prime time for me to learn from Pete's life experiences as I did in the past. This was my moment to pass my tough test. My heart would always tell me "you KNOW this isn't right." My flesh would say "just one last time." Men, it's very simple but does take time to conceive. Your inner conviction or feeling must overcome and override your flesh(physical craving for pornography, prostitution, etc.).It is a constant battle between the two. We will discuss this in great detail later.

I have no knowledge of the condition of Pete's life today. Since then hopefully and prayerfully things have worked out for his best. It just shows that if you decide to stand as a man to fight your life battles, be prepared to fight to stay out of sexual addiction. It always, always, always starts small. Good or bad, right or wrong, ANYTHING YOU FEED WILL GROW. Anything. It's the same with sex…the seductive addiction.

"HIDDEN AGENDA"

One Thursday night a couple of friends and I decided to go out to get something to eat. I was single at the time and this was something I did often. Two to three nights per week were normal for me, but this night would be different.

I would frequent go-go bars (as you know by now) on a weekly basis. Even at lunch time. It was a hidden place where I could secretly fulfill my lustful desires while escaping from my responsibilities. This wicked cycle caused me financial pain as well as emotional pain. As my friends drove up to the bar (mind you we totally skipped dinner), I felt a sense of uneasiness. I did not know what it was at the time.

The four of us sat down. I was on the far end of the bar. I remember looking at my drink and saying to myself "this place is miserable. I can't wait to get out of here." As soon as I thought this, my friend yelled to me "Hey Sanford, this dancer says she knows you." I looked and said with a hint of arrogance, "she can't possibly know me." The girl motioned for me to come near her. " Sanford, you used to live on South 19ᵗʰ street. Isn't Mrs. Ashley your mother? She taught at Madison Avenue School. It's me! Debra!

Gulp. There I was, called out in front of my friends. My heart sank. I felt exposed to my friends, my mother and Debra. My secret life was finally out in the open. That was my last night ever in a go-go bar. In retrospect, I learned that WHATEVER IS DONE IN THE DARK WILL BE EXPOSED IN THE LIGHT!! Period.

My exposure came through a go-go dancer. Another man's exposure may be unleashed at a restaurant accompanied by a woman who is not his wife. They both may be seen in an "intimate position" with each other. A single man can really maneuver in a clandestine fashion. He does not have a wife, so he is virtually not accountable to anyone for his actions or "social activities". I can guarantee you this: everything that is done will be exposed at some point and time. What were the chances of me going to a go-go bar and being called out by a former neighbor? Even worse, someone who knew my own mother? Think about that. Hidden agenda's come with a hefty price tag. The price can be loss of your marriage, health, public scrutiny, unemployment, etc. The question you must ask yourself is not if I will pay the price, but WHEN I will pay the price. You can pay on the front end, which is immediate recognition of the problem, dealing with it, getting help, and moving on. You can pay on the back end, where you reap the unfortunate circumstances of job loss, divorce, SEXUALLY TRANSMITTED DISEASES, etc. Men, you hold the checkbook. At some point, if you do not address this addiction, you will have a price to pay. Trust me.

"EXCUSES,EXCUSES,EXCUSES"

I speak frequently at men's groups, churches, retreats, etc. What I find as the most common denominator among men with this secret life is excuses. Excuses, excuses, excuses. It simply amazes me of how men simply waste so much time to conjure up excuses, especially for our sexual escapades. Excuses are color coated maskings of the truth. It's like putting a band aid on an open sore. You cover up the sore, but you did not treat it, so it can heal. The root of the sore is still infected and untreated. You are just covering up the problem.

One of the excuses I hear is that "it was something that just happened." So let me get this straight. You just happened to go to a video store and just happened to pick up an x-rated movie to take home. You just happened to put it in your DVD or VCR player and you just happened to view it. Wait, here is a better one. After you watched it you just happened to go out and solicit a prostitute. She just happened to perform a sexual act on you then you went about your merry way.

Well. Let me break this to you as gently as I can and with truth. None of this "just happened". Are there any pockets of your life that just happened? Did you receive your high school diploma or college degree by chance? Did that just happen? Or were you intentional about going to school faithfully everyday and studying hard? Your goal was probably to obtain the best education possible, to obtain the best job possible, to maximize your earnings potential. So if I or any other man opts to go out and sleep with a prostitute; or if someone goes out and molests a young child....it has happened by choice. Not circumstances. NOTHING JUST HAPPENS.

There are root causes that trigger our choices, including sexual choices. There is also a payday that comes with these choices. You will always reap what you sow. Always. Your actions and behavior determine how you are going to pay.

Excuses are extremely costly and cause trouble. Fear is one of the prime motivators of making excuses. Fear is simply something that is false that appears to be real. It is falsehood. Fear stifles us from moving forward. Fear keeps us from a healthy and wealthy life. It is the blessing blocker. It is when excuses are fear based that the truth is suppressed. Most of the time we know the truth. We tend to know what is right and wrong. That is why so many people enjoy sexual addiction because it gives them a thrill. The thrill of not getting caught drives a sex addict to see just how far he can go before the penalty catches up with him.

Solomon was a man who made an excuse for his sexual addiction. Known to many as "the wise man", Solomon actually loved many, many women. He actually had seven hundred wives and three hundred concubines. His story can be found in the Bible in I Kings 2,versus 1-13.As time grew Solomon became more engrossed in his sin. He married women who represented and worshipped other gods. This caused Solomon to turn his Heart from God. This resulted in

Solomon's downward spiral. God became angry with Solomon and told him since he has turned his heart from Him(God),He would tear the kingdom away from Solomon. Solomon kept his womanizing. Since he did not follow God's instruction to stop, God DID tear the kingdom away from Solomon. God did this but not during Solomon's lifetime. God tore the kingdom out of Solomon's son's hand instead!!

What happened here? First of all Solomon simply excused his sexual addiction to women. He went and married and slept with these women KNOWING that he was not supposed to. Secondly, in verse six the Bible shows that Solomon did know the difference between right and wrong. Verse six states that Solomon did evil according to God and did not follow Him "completely." It's evident that Solomon still knew where God stood with this. Solomon simply excused God's instruction as well. Thirdly, God did(and always) keeps His word. He tore the kingdom away from Solomon's son. Solomon's legacy, purpose and destiny would fall short due to sexual addiction.

Solomon was the wisest man to ever live. He was a wealthy man. He was a trader, diplomat, the third king of Israel. Solomon helped build God's temple in Jerusalem. His leadership and position of influence was affected by his lust for sexual gratification. The women he married and the women he slept with influenced his thinking and his actions. Solomon did learn his lesson late in life. Please read the book of Ecclesiates in the Bible. Solomon's grief and pain is well scripted there.

“WHAT'S NEXT?”

There are many mavericks in the world who could care less about getting help with sexual addiction. Some men could care less about their families and the effect this has on them. But there are those who are reading this and say “I get it Sanford. So what do I do next?”

I have been where a lot of you men are now. I want to help you. First, sit down somewhere quiet to pull out a pad or piece of paper. Write down what you are sexually addicted to. You know what it is…pornography, massage parlors, beastiality, internet porn, whatever. Look at that list real good. Now think of the big goal(s) and desires that you have. Write these down on the paper next to your addictions. There is a direct correlation to your sexual addictions and to the desires and goals that you're trying to reach. I can tell you this because this is what I lived with for over ten years….delayed destiny.

Next we will discuss the roots of this addiction. You are going to find what triggers you to go and act out. The most important thing is to know that freedom from this is a PROCESS.DON'T GET DISCOURAGED!! Progress is more important than perfection. Anything that is monitored or measured will vastly improve. Since you have purchased this book I know you mean business. Let's jump into the next chapter to get to the root of this so you can claim the prize that awaits you.

CHAPTER TWO

The Root

My perspective of what a man is has changed significantly over the years. Men that I deem as "solid" men are men that have integrity and honesty. They are not afraid of responsibility and love their families wholeheartedly. These men get involved in their communities, are mentors to others and influence other people. These are observations I have made from my personal life. My male friendships range from truck drivers to a chairman of a well known U.S company. I am not boasting of my association with these men. I am simply showing you that job title does not qualify who you are. Your CHARACTER determines who you are.

Always develop your "character root". Character is your calling card. Strong character will protect you from a very destructive root called dissatisfaction.

Roots are at the bottom of our core selves. We say constantly "What's the root of the problem? What is the cause? What character trait causes an outward action which reaps great results or bad results?"

Dissatisfaction is one of the roots that can be good or bad. One can become dissatisfied with various societal concerns. By starting a foundation to fund and aid those afflicted by drugs, homelessness, racism, poverty, etc; one can use this dissatisfaction in a positive sense.

It's pretty alarming how many people are dissatisfied with their lives. Instead of being thankful for what they do have, they murmur and gripe about what they don't have. Dissatisfaction and disappointment for the most part go hand in hand. The two are sometimes connected. When we are satisfied with our lives, we deem ourselves blessed. We are happy. Work is great. Home is great. We are on top of the world....invincible. Unfortunately, this false sense of invincibility often causes us to start to make plans and decisions without any type of guidance. We think we have the answer to everything, and we don't want anyone to suggest anything to us.

When our plans become disappointments, we become dissatisfied. This can be a point where the birth of sexual addiction takes place. How? It's very simple. We feel that we are owed something to compensate for our dissatisfaction with the various outcomes in our lives. Many of these outcomes are based on our own decisions we've made. We may feel we should have a certain type of woman, or one that looks a certain way. We see the outside of this woman, not knowing what the inside is like. So we go for the next best thing. We look for websites full of women. Porn sites, magazines, peep shows, you name it. Because we feel these things will satisfy us we are willing to justify our pursuit of them. There are three key things that can keep you from falling into this deceitful trap. It will work for you, but you must apply these principles.

1. STOP COVETING AND COMPARING YOURSELVES TO OTHERS.

Being complacent and comfortable is different from being content. Content is being happy in the state that you are in. Be thankful for who you are, where you are. Don't look at others situations and compare them to yours. You have no clue what is going on in their lives. Let your situations motivate you to make progress daily in your own life. Jealousy and comparative competing will defeat you….every time!!

2. BE PATIENT AND NOT IMPULSIVE.

Whatever disappointments you face, be patient and do not over react like a person out of control. Don't be impulsive. Quickly look at what went wrong or what is currently going wrong; analyze it, and address it. DON'T BURY YOUR FEELINGS!! If your dissatisfaction consumes you it will be masqueraded through sexually addictive actions.

3. BUILD A BRIDGE TO THE NEW ROAD.

The fact that you can work, live, dine, and worship where you want should make you very appreciative of your life. Yes, there is always that bigger home or boat, or another job promotion. These things are fine when kept in complete balance. The fact that these things are not in your possession does not mean anyone owes you anything. Concentrate on character and these things will chase you down. Dissatisfaction will then be a thing of the past.

ANGER

Jeffrey works 55-60 hours per week. He comes home from work everyday, says hello to his family and gets comfortable. His wife Sara is an at home mom. She has spent all day running the household. They have three kids. Sara does everything from entertaining the kids to running errands like food shopping, gardening and preparing lunch. It is a job within itself.(AT HOME MOMS...I SALUTE YOU!!).

Recently Sara has been getting overwhelmed with it all. Part of her daily routine was to have dinner ready by the time Jeffrey comes home. With all of the work that goes on at the house, she has been cooking dinner after Jeffrey gets home.

Jeffrey is starting to dislike this routine. Instead of asking his wife why this is starting to happen, he starts to discuss his anger and frustration with his work buddies. He confides in them instead of talking openly with his wife. This goes on for a decent amount of time. Jeffrey finally decides to tell his wife of his discontent. Sara snaps back and tells him she simply does not have the time sometimes, and how come he does not help her at home? At this point Jeffrey should have put on his "Husband Hat". Jeffrey could have simply said "Honey, how can I help you? I know all day you have been working non-stop. What can I do to help?"

Since Jeffrey does not do this, and both Sara and Jeffrey are burying their feelings.......nothing gets resolved. Resentment starts to set in and Jeffrey is becoming very, very angry. Jeffrey starts to confide more in his work buddies. One day his buddies invite him out after work for a drink to release his anger. The drinks after work start to escalate and become Jeffrey's new routine. Jeffrey starts to think that since he provides for his family and works 55-60 hours per week, he is entitled to more rewards. His buddies invited him to a nude bar one day after work. This also became routine to the tune of 3-4 nights per week! Jeffry is now missing out on family time, and not to mention dinner.

After a few months of missing payments on house bills, Jeffrey finally told Sara what he was doing, and why he was doing it. It took a long time for Sara to get over the hurt. He explained that he was so angry that he "felt like doing something about this." Their marriage was restored, but not after some serious trust building between the two.

We see what happens when anger is suppressed along with buried feelings. We can become walking time bombs. Sex brings brief gratification and temporarily takes away anger. Sex was created to be a pleasurable experience between man and wife, but society uses it as a power tool. If there is any anger in a marriage, it will manifest itself in the bedroom. It can block true intimacy. It is detrimental to a person who does not know how to channel their anger. It is an emotion that we all have. Anger channeled in the right direction can bring good results. Bad or bitter anger gets pulled out from its root because of the positive direction that good anger takes. Let me explain.

My anger was developed from frustration and disappointment in my career and other personal issues. I was not thankful for what I had accomplished in my life at the time. I was not even thankful for all of the great things I had at that time. I was not married and did not have a girlfriend so it was very easy for me to wallow in my sexual addiction. I was very angry at my past relationships with women. I never dealt with anger from the many relationships that went sour. Every ounce of anger simply built up over the years. My first marriage failed miserably and was a mistake from the start. I made it my goal not to ever get involved in a serious relationship ever again, and I meant it. The anger and resentment I had caused me to seek out places and people to fill the emotional void in my life.

After 10 years I finally cried out to God for help and got it. I was finally free from this addiction. No more massage parlors, go-go bars, you name it and it was finished! Then, I got really angry. Every time I thought of the debt I had accumulated, the money I had lost, the car that had been taken back by the bank; it was enough. I got very angry. This "good anger" fueled me to look for a better job, and truly seek out my purpose in life. I expected to recoup all that I had lost due to this addiction. I was determined to make a change in my life.

Get a grip on the anger root. You CONTROL IT. Write out why you are angry. Confront the anger and confront yourself. Why lose out on so much in life due to anger and sexual addiction?

LUST

Malcolm and I got a chance to speak before our men's group meeting with each other. We have been personal friends for many, many years. We know each other very, very well. "Sanford, I just can't take it. Latin women are so sexy. The way they dress, the way they act, and talk. I am so attracted to them. I can't stop thinking about them!!

At this time Malcolm was going through some struggles in his marriage. If he was to achieve total victory and restoration in his marriage, he could not afford to fall into any type of temptation. I asked Malcolm if he thought a lustful comment like that was appropriate for a woman outside of his wife. I told Malcolm that these thoughts can be brought into existence if he does not banish them. Malcolm replied, "It's just a thought. How can that cause a problem?"

One week later, Malcolm was given an assignment at work which required a new team member. He and his workmate met for meetings, then lunch, and eventually after work. His new teammate was a woman...a Latino woman.

Ninety percent of their meetings were discussions about each other and not work. Malcolm eluded to the fact that he simply adored Latin women. Daily his co-worker would dress in an alluring manner. Malcom's co-workers started to take notice of the two's inappropriate friendliness to each other.

Despite this tumultuous emotional affair, Malcolm was spared the devastation of falling into sexual temptation. I informed Malcolm to tell his wife immediately what had been going on. He did tell his wife and the affair has ceased. Actually, the woman was transferred within days of him telling his wife; and their marriage is well on its way back to marital bliss. Most of all, Malcolm set boundaries on his thought life. We will discuss boundaries later.

Now Malcolm was spared, but there are many who fall flat on their face with this root constantly. Lustful thoughts are generated by something we see, hear or touch. The image that you are lusting after can stay in your mind for a very long time. This image causes you to be aroused since it is embedded in your mind. The more time you focus on that image, the more you are inclined to lust. Once you have lustfully looked, you have already committed a lustful act in your mind.

If the root of lust is not challenged, lust can possibly lead to stalking, sexual harassment, even rape. We have seen numerous athletes, entertainers and corporate executives get caught and chastised publicly for their sexual exploits. Even this morning a former athlete was arrested in a foreign country for committing an act of sexual harassment. He has been incarcerated before for the same type of crime. When this happens, a person's character and reputation are tarnished. Despite all of their achievements and accolades, the sex crimes that they committed are what they will probably be remembered for most.

The root of lust is the deadliest of them all. We will discuss how to pull this root out of you shortly.

DISTANT DAD

As I stated earlier, the late Clarence Ashley Jr.(my dad) was the epitome of manhood to me. My mother, the late Ellen Ashley was truly a remarkable woman. Both of my parents were always there for each other and us as well. I don't take the short time my father was on this earth for granted.(He died when he was 49 years young).My father exhibited commitment, honesty, integrity and discipline. These traits were deposited in me at an early age. Everyday my father kissed my mother before he went to work. He would always tell her that he loved her. Every morning I do the same to my wife.

There are scores of men who never had a father. Some men may have had fathers whose character traits were not that good. Their fathers may have been alcoholics, lazy, or woman chasers. These dads maybe weren't loyal to family, friends, co-workers, no one. A deep void is left in a man whose dad is "distant". Emotional, physical, and social distance from a father to a son can lead to a longing for fatherly love. There is a need that a boy has to see how to love and treat his wife. If a dad does not connect with his wife and his son, the son will model manhood from outside the home. It is direction that the son craves for. The son wants to know how to treat a woman from dating to marriage.

The media infuses sexual images constantly. Media shows that the more women a man has, the more of a man he is. Whatever a man thinks of himself, he will surely become. A dad who is up close and personal with his son can protect him from this onslaught of sexual persuasion. If the dad is modeling love and faithfulness to his wife, you can rest assured that the son will pattern himself the same way. Respect your wife, and your son will respect his wife. If you glance at a woman who is not your wife, he will peek as well.

The son ALWAYS looks for approval from his dad. He wants to know he is a young man growing into manhood. He wants to know that he has what it takes to be a man. Sexuality is included in this. He wants to know what to do when Susie keeps flirting with him. It is YOUR responsibility as a dad to show him and lead him down the right path. When the root of the distant dad is not dealt with, it can carry over to the adult life of a man. He will then seek to be wanted and approved by women sexually. If he feels that he can satisfy her sexually, then that constitutes to him that he is a man. As we stated earlier, the more women he has, the more he sees himself as a man.

I have spoken with scores and scores of men who have this root so deeply embedded in them that are crying for help. The distant dad root is a very somber topic to discuss. If a man is going to excel in all areas of life, this root has to be confronted head on. If this wound manifests men will be torn by warped emotions that will lead to sexual addiction. They will seek affirmation and approval from women sexually without making any type of commitment to that woman.

PULLING THE DISTANT DAD ROOT

Healing the distant dad wound can be very painful emotionally. Yet, it can also be the most liberating thing that you will ever do!! Here are some practical steps that if they are applied will have you on your to way restoration.

1.FORGIVE YOUR FATHER FOR WHATEVER HE DID….NOW!!

This is a tough one. You may not be in contact with your dad. Maybe you never have even met him. No matter how you may feel, you must understand that forgiveness is FOR YOU! It is about you setting yourself free of any bitterness or anger towards your dad. Un-forgiveness keeps you from moving forward in your life. If your father has moved on in his life, shouldn't you as well?

2.MEET YOUR DAD FACE TO FACE AND TELL HIM HOW YOU FEEL.

If your dad is alive, set up a time to meet. Breakfast or lunch is ideal to have a man to man conversation. Speak with respect, yet be firm and fair. Let your dad honestly know how you feel about him being distant. There is a great chance that he has no idea what you have been feeling for years. Give him the benefit of the doubt by allowing him to explain himself. If your dad is deceased or not physically available, write a "letter" to him. Get out a legal pad and put exactly how you feel on paper. Let every ounce of emotion out of you. Pour it on the paper. There will be great emotional release in this. Once this letter is written, you must let go. Discard the letter or if you can mail it to him. It will be tough at first, but if it takes twenty pages to be released, so be it. Once you forgive, LET IT GO!!!

LIES

It was our first date. It was an awesome October day. I scheduled time off from work so that I could be with this beautiful woman. As we started to exit off the parkway, I began to discuss my past with Mona(my date). I have known Mona all my life. We were always friends, but this was different. This was a date. It was a big step to becoming more acquainted.

I shared my past with Mona...the past she didn't know about. Discussing my involvement with masturbation, massage parlors, and go-go bars was not what I had in mind. I knew I could not lie to her. I knew this discussion would happen at some point. I have always wanted to be with Mona. If we were going to date, I knew that I was at some point going to marry her. If there was any trial test on my ability to tell the truth, this was definitely it!!

Mona listened to me with such grace, empathy and ever so lovingly. I had peace after I shared my secret. My transparency at that moment has become the key to our marriage...honesty.

Secrets and lies are like weeds in a garden. One secret will spread into a garden of just weeds. A weed must be pulled at its root in order to allow beautiful flowers to appear. By being open and honest with your mate, you will ensure a beautiful garden.

Lies are a strong root. The more lies you tell, the stronger the root grows. In turn, the tougher it is to remove. Lies are the ultimate root of sexual addiction. It becomes a habit that can destroy you.

My friend Dan had it bad. I mean it was pretty bad. I have known this man for well over twenty five years. When we were kids, Dan always tried to make himself supreme to me in practically everything we did.(Except in academics, he could not touch me there!).Dan always had the latest sneakers first, even though he never wore them. Dan was a high school athlete. Dan was always the guy who scored three touchdowns in a football game, and pumped in thirty points in a basketball game. Yet when we looked in the local paper to look at his stats, we always found something different than what he said. Oh yes, Dan did score. He just scored one touchdown versus three. As for basketball he scored as well. Dan only scored seven points in the game; usually late in the fourth quarter.

Dan's fables did not stop at high school. Dan started dating and boy did he enjoy himself. Dan had fun lying and mistreating women all throughout high school. He used and abused them. His lies just seemed to grow more and more.

Dan went on to college where the charades continued. College was a whirlwind of deceit. Dan made his college football team by being awarded a four year scholarship. This only added fuel to the fire. Dan did not wait to start meeting girls on campus, lie to them and sleep with them. He told all of them he was single and he was not "fooling around with anyone."

Weekends meant trouble for Dan. By Thursday, he would receive five to six messages from women wanting to know what plans he had for them this weekend. Dan had to constantly scramble for new lies to cover the different scenarios he painted for each woman. Dan loved when his team played in other cities because it became easier to meet new women. These women were located too far to make a commitment, which suited Dan fine.(It was amazing how many women agreed to this arrangement.)

These lies did not cease. As Dan progressed in all areas of his life, so did his lies. Dan's character greatly diminished. Dan hardly ever told the truth now. His friends and family were at a point that no one knew if we could believe anything Dan said!! Dan had a different woman with him every time we saw him. He would always tell us of his sexual exploits with each one.

One thing I learned from Dan is this: nothing goes unseen and unaccounted for. At some point, you will pay a hefty price for sexual addiction. You either pay now...or you pay later. You make the decision to when you pay and what will you pay with. If you choose to take the better path, and you pay with commitment and truth, you will be blessed with a great girlfriend or spouse. Your wife will fulfill your needs and more! Pay with transparency and you will be used to accomplish mighty things in life.

Unfortunately, you never know what you will have to pay with. You risk health, finances, guilt, shame, etc. You will have a ¼ cup of life instead of a full one. Why would you want a life that is short of what it could be?

Dan's lies did catch up with him. One young woman he co-habited with found out about another woman he was seeing and literally threw him and his clothes out on the street! She broke off the relationship immediately. Dan found a small apartment to live in until he met another woman. He informed this woman about his "extensive" college education. The young lady shortly afterwards ran into a neighbor who had just met Dan at a train station. Both ladies were discussing how they met a "great guy" named Dan. Both ladies stopped seeing Dan.

Dan did finally get it. He finally gave up his free -wheeling sex life and addiction. He got serious and started a new action plan. He spent time with men who were made of strong moral fiber. They helped Dan set big goals for his life. He was now accountable to someone other than himself. Within two years Dan received two promotions at his job. He also got married and is now enjoying his two beautiful daughters!! Dan is enjoying a healthy and wealthy life.

Turnarounds take time, but there is victory that awaits you when you do change. Lies are vicious. They hold us back from being all we can be, and doing all we can do in life. The more you are capable of telling the truth, the more peace you will have. You can live a life looking ahead, not constantly looking behind you.

If you remember nothing else about the root of lies, please try to remember this……….

L=LETTING
I=INCIDENTS THAT ARE FABRICATED
E=ERASE YOUR
S=SUCCESS

CHAPTER THREE

Boundaries....Protecting the Fortress

As I walked across the tradeshow floor, I spotted a vendor booth that had a golf putting green. I decided to go over and try to put a few balls in. There were two men in front of me. We all started talking. One of the men and I really connected well.

We discussed business, the trade show and our personal lives. The young man was recently engaged and was scheduled to be married next year. I strongly felt the need to share my dating period with my wife, which lasted 2 ½ years. I explained how we both agreed to be abstinent this time period. We wanted to purify and purge ourselves of all the past junk that we had and to start all over. My wife and I became so close emotionally and spiritually. It was this time that we got clear direction for our lives. Our purposes were defined through this time period as well.

I also let the gentlemen know how difficult it was to really abstain from sex at this time. We had to set up strong boundaries around ourselves. After a date, I would leave Mona's house at a reasonable hour, so that we would not slip up on our abstinence period.

A very interesting thing happened. After I closed my time of sharing, this young man started to weep. "It has been so hard for us to be celibate. We have been trying for the same reasons that you did. I have really, really struggled but now I know it can be done."

I explained to the young man what I am going to explain to you. A boundary is merely a fence, border, or box that you set around you to keep you from any type of harm. A fortress may have guardsman at the gate to protect the fort from intruders. A garden has a fence that protects anyone from harming plants or vegetables by stepping on them. Your house is protected by a property border so neighbors won't step on your property without your permission.

Boundaries are permissive. It is on your watch. You have the ability to keep things from over stepping their boundaries. While dating my wife, I left her house early enough that I would not be tempted do anything with her sexually. I know myself pretty, pretty well. If I would have stayed later in the night at her house, I would have definitely tried something!! Many will read this part and say that I am going overboard. I am simply stating what has worked for me and my wife, and we have been richly rewarded for it.

Boundaries are something you must set and be firm with. Boundaries are designed to protect us emotionally and physically. An emotional boundary can be some CD you have at home and every time you play it, you cry. This was your ex-girlfriend's favorite song. It just rips you emotionally every time you play it. Do yourself a favor: either stop playing it or get rid of it. Set an emotional boundary by not even having access to the CD. Playing it again and again will not bring her back. You have got to move on.

Boundaries keep garbage out of our lives. The best way to visualize this is to think of the garbage can in your house. Now I know this sounds simple, but this is exactly why I am using this example. I am quite sure that your kitchen garbage can is lined with a garbage bag. This bag is used to store garbage and protect anyone from harmful, detrimental germs. It is no good for you. The garbage bag is the boundary between you and the garbage. Sexual addiction is the garbage and proper boundaries will keep this addiction out of your life.

Are you with me? Good. When your garbage can becomes full, the obvious and practical thing to do is to remove the bag. You take the bag out of your house to your trash can. If you don't remove the trash, you will soon smell a foul stench of garbage in your house.

It is the same with sexual addiction. The addiction to porn, prostitution, peep shows, etc., will contaminate other areas of your life. Your finances, your family, relationships and other areas will become infected by the stench of sexual addiction. Sexual addiction may be odorless to you, but it travels through the crevices of our lives; causing all types of discomfort. It causes divorces, failed businesses, and sexually transmitted diseases to name a few.

Boundaries separate and protect you from everything you have stewardship over. You must keep that perspective to avoid falling into the sweet trap of sexual addiction.

Think about this: when you take out the garbage, what do you do ?You leave the garbage outside. All of it. Do you go out and dig back into the garbage for a chicken bone or empty carton of milk? Of course not!! It is the same with sexual addiction. You can't say to yourself, " Okay, this is my last pornographic tape. I am done. I will stop right now." As you are throwing out your porno videos, you stumble upon an old porno magazine. Now what will you do with it? Will you part with it or keep it hidden somewhere for a quick fix later? Will you step up to it as the man that you are and throw it out with the rest of the garbage? If there is anything in your house, car, office, garage, tool shed, or mechanic shop that is pornographic….get rid of it!! These possessions will keep you locked up in this cesspool of sexual addiction.

Boundaries will protect and preserve you. With every condition there is a promise. You will always reap what you sow. Sow is the condition, reap is the promise. You will always have a way of escape and boundaries can help facilitate that. You must be willing to be open to the escape routes, and run through them!!

Let's look at some other ways to create and keep safe effective boundaries.

BOUNDARY #1 = "Mind Matters"

What matters to the mind is what is put in the mind. If pure, clean thoughts are put into the mind,

34

then what these thoughts produce will matter. Family will matter, your community service will matter, health, relationships, and success will matter if that is what your mind is focused on. Nothing else will matter.

If sexual thoughts from internet porn sites, phone sex, and virtual sex occurs, you will register those thoughts and images. The more the mind concentrates on those thoughts, those thoughts will matter.

Literature you read, songs that you may hear that are lyrically suggestive will take your mind beyond what you hear or see. Your mind operates like a funnel. What goes in must come out. So here is a step to create a mental boundary. It does take time, but in the end it is well, well worth doing.

SEXUAL THOUGHTS= SEXUAL ACTIONS
= SEXUAL ADDICTIVE ACTIONS

POSITIVE PURE THOUGHTS = POSITIVE
ACTIONS = POSITIVE RESULTS

Remember that we are talking about sexual addiction. This addiction starts very small. It is the "backdoor addiction." You never see it coming because it starts out harmless and bears no affect. This addiction mushrooms. You must renew your mind daily. Focus and fix it on progressive pure thoughts. Your actions are triggered mentally and that is why I wanted to make sure we started here first. Since you will master this boundary and apply it, let's prepare you for the next boundary.

BOUNDARY # 2 = "Body to Body"

This boundary is vital. You must put your body in "boundary mode" at all times. You never know when temptation will strike. You may be in the most strangest of places and you will have to pull this one out to keep from falling. Let me show you.

I was on a flight on business from Newark Airport to Phoenix, Arizona. As I arrived in Phoenix, I had totally forgotten about the time difference. I felt sluggish. As I checked into my hotel, I decided to have my bags sent to my room. I headed straight to the restaurant for dinner.

As I got up the next morning I noticed I had overslept by about thirty minutes. Since I am big on time management, this really upset me. I was starving so in order to save time I called in breakfast to be delivered to my room. I sometimes will do this with dinner to resist eating in a lounge, which may make me privy to temptation. I frantically jumped into the shower, came out and pulled out my clothes to pick my suit for the day.

Suddenly, there was a knock on my door. I looked through the door to see a woman delivering my breakfast. I had almost forgot about breakfast. " I will be right there, let me grab a shirt" I said. As soon as I opened the door, the woman's eyes suggestively locked with mine. I asked her to come in, yet I was somewhat uncomfortable. As she sat my breakfast down she said "It was ok to come to the door without your shirt. Maybe I should leave and come in again." My response was "I think you should leave now."

Now this was a prime opportunity to make a critical decision. I chose the right one. No one, absolutely no one would have found out about this. I was thousands of miles away from New Jersey. I had just started dating my wife at that time. I strongly think that I would not be writing this book for you had I made the wrong decision. My situation required me to act and act quickly, or I could have been in deep trouble. I would have run out of the room if I had to.

The body to body boundary is designed to keep your body at a safe distance with any woman that you may come in contact with. While conducting business at work, you may have developed a great working relationship with a female employee. It is strictly a business relationship. Physical touching such as "playful hugging", suggestive flirting(or any kind of flirting),or even "friendly kissing" should be avoided. You send the wrong signal to the woman, and if you are married all of these actions need to be reserved for your wife only.

Yes, I understand at holiday parties a kiss on the cheek will happen wishing one a pleasant holiday. I understand that. But when there is constant physical contact, you are opening up a serious doorway to other activities.

Keep your distance at all times physically. If you are the least bit attracted to a woman who you think that you will possibly "fall for", put up the fences around you!! For those men that travel, please apply this boundary. Remember Dan earlier in the book who traveled with his football team? He had a woman for every city he set his foot in. Resist, resist, resist!!

Emotional distance is just as important as physical distance. That's why boundary number three is equally important.

BOUNDARY # 3 = "Relational Reluctance"

Relationships are vital to everyday living. Can you imagine if relationships were never formed? Relationships help us from accomplishing goals to gaining solid wisdom on the relevant issues in life. Women are very much relational and emotional. Men are wired to be conquerors, leaders, warriors, and some of us mavericks. Men like to be heroes and women like to be rescued. Men have this strange tendency to think that we know everything!!!(Go ahead ladies, laugh while you can).Men also believe that when it comes to solving problems, we have all the answers to those problems. I call it "authoritative arrogance". Some men have this so bad that they are totally oblivious to the subtle attacks; which can lead to sexual addiction. If you are not careful, it can happen to you, too.

Bill found this out for himself. He has been married for twenty five years to his wife Susan. They are both the proud parents of two teenage girls. Bill had always been a faithful man as a father, provider, encourager, and leader in the family's home. He is involved in his community, his church, and coaches a local boys baseball team.

Bill heads up the marketing department at the company he works for. Due to expansion in certain markets, Bill was asked to come into work a little earlier and leave later. There were a few new team members added to help facilitate all of the new changes. The accounting department had most of the new people, since the sales were forecasted to go through the roof.

As Bill went to go and get a cup of coffee at the vending machine, he noticed a tall lean woman who was having problems with the machine. She had pushed a couple of the wrong buttons on the machine. Bill walked over, showed her how to work the machine, and she walked back to her office. Bill looked at the woman as she walked away.

The next day, Bill went again to get coffee only to find the same woman at the machine. It seemed that they both had the same coffee time. Bill formally introduced himself to the woman. The two of them started talking and next thing you know they were past their break time. They both scurried back to their offices. Soon this "coffee time" developed into a daily habit for the two of them. The woman and Bill started discussing non-work related issues such as his marriage, her career, her ex-boyfriend, etc.

Soon the woman started visiting Bill at his office. She loved talking to Bill, because he would always listen to her; her problems, her thoughts, dreams, etc. Bill would constantly try to give advice to her. He of course has all the answers to all her problems.(So he thinks).

Many co-workers started to notice the "new relationship" Bill was in. His bosses really started to frown upon the relationship. Bill of course did not find anything wrong. He just saw himself as someone to help her with her transitions in life. According to Bill, he has done nothing wrong. Except one thing: he has not told his wife about his new buddy.

Bill was working late one night and this woman came by his office to say goodnight. He asked her how things were going and she immediately started pouring out her problems to him. Bill invited her to sit down.

The woman starts to cry uncontrollably. Bill runs around to the other side of the desk to give her a facial tissue. He puts his arm around her and the woman quickly returns the favor. Then the woman plants a kiss right on Bill's lips. Bill, to his surprise returned the favor. As you might guess, one thing led to another and the two had a sexual encounter. Bill had just fallen into a sexual sin because of the emotional adultery he had been committing along the way.

Bill eventually told his wife of the affair. His casual boundary-less affair ripped through his wife and his kids. His daughters became very distant emotionally and physically from their dad. They always saw dad as a man that was different from all the other guys. Now his girls looked at him as "just like any other man." Bill and Susan eventually divorced, leaving the entire family in emotional disarray.

There were safeguards and boundaries that Bill could have put in place. The first mistake he made was that he glanced at this woman upon her departure from the vending machine. His look evidently registered a thought that stayed in his mind that made him become curious about her. He did not realize it. RULE # 1…..
DON'T GLANCE.

Secondly, when his coffee times were starting to constantly coincide with hers, he should have made a change. It sounds radical, but if you want to beat this(sexual addiction) you have got to be radical. Bill could have taken his coffee break earlier or later, but he obviously did not want to. A ten to fifteen minute coffee break would not hurt a soul. As we see in this case, not changing his coffee times did hurt a few souls.

Thirdly, Bill should have been reluctant to have anything more than a business relationship with this woman. Sure you will have conversations when your co-workers will want to find out some things about you. This is normal. That's why I always mention that I am married right upfront in my first casual conversation. Bill should have done the same thing. He could have steered the conversations to team projections, company memos, products, etc. He opened an emotional gate to his heart(and hers) by having emotion based conversations with her.

Lastly, telling his wife of this new addition to his team would have made her feel very secure. Susan would have saw that through his openness that she was his only true love; and he was not thinking of anyone else. This makes our wives trust us even more. Transparency brings comfort, peace, and trust into any relationship.

It is great to help someone who is in distress and needs help. But we must exercise wisdom and discernment so that we will not fall into a pattern of sexual addiction as a result. Relational reluctance will help you keep safe emotional and physical boundaries from others that will cause you to fall. If you find yourself the least bit attracted to another woman(especially if you are married) that can lead down the wrong road. Distance yourself. For the most part, men know which women are attracted to them as much as being attracted to that woman. Bill never confronted himself about the emotional attraction that he had for this woman. He wanted to be her hero, answer all her questions and be there for her. The problem was that he did it for the wrong woman. Bill did it for the wrong woman. Men, do it for your wives or girlfriend. Protect them emotionally and physically. Make sure the woman you are committed to gets 110% of you. Nothing less!!

Boundary # 4 = "Guarding The Gates"

Bill was a prime example of what a glance can produce. The eyes are a powerful magnet. What your eyes register and capture will paint photos of various images. The eyes function very much as a camera. The same principles that apply to the mind go for the eyes. If you intake "garbage" visually, the graphic images will stay in and on your mind. That is why pornographic magazines are so effective. Some men view them so much that they see air brushed harlots constantly in their mind. This can interfere in a marriage because in intimate times with his wife, the husband may start to think of those women he saw in the magazine. Some men have gotten so far into the addiction that they can't make love to their wife. The wife in turn feels shame and guilt. The wife then feels that she is not attractive or loved by her husband. Women- please know this: if your husband is caught in sexual addiction, there is a good chance that you are not the cause. Don't let your hubby try to sell you that!! He simply needs to take ownership for his behavior.

Men are extremely visual. Women are very emotional. Men tend to focus on various things, but one thing at a time intently. When I hear the term "tunnel vision", I almost immediately think of this as a masculine term. Tunnel vision describes leaders, athletes, executives, etc. Not all men live by tunnel vision. See, tunnel vision is just that: viewing everything from one lens. I used to be one that would always say that I am driven by my tunnel vision. I stopped that immediately after I discovered that tunnel vision makes you privy to a ton of blind spots. These spots are danger points that you can't see if you are only looking through a tunnel. When you focus on the porno movie you just saw, the blind spots around the tunnel are the images that stay with you. When you and your wife are cuddling together in your bedroom, ALL OF YOUR ATTENTION SHOULD BE ON HER,NOT THE WOMAN YOU JUST SAW IN THE VIDEO LAST NIGHT. The blind spot is that you had no clue that what you saw in the video would distract you from being intimate with your wife!! Men with no vision perish, but men with tunnel vision are dangerous to themselves and others.

Women do use the term tunnel vision as well. There are women that struggle with sexual addiction as well. Women are definitely more emotional. (Have you ever gone to a romantic comedy movie on a date? Try it. You will definitely agree with me!!)I believe that women have the distinct advantage of being more broad based in that they are able to focus on more than one thing at a time. Men tend to be task oriented by focusing on one thing at a time.

The gates of the eyes are vital sense we obviously need and depend on vision for our every day lives. When you are stuck in sexual addiction, it makes it very difficult to fight off the visual images you see daily. Everywhere you go there is a "bait trap" set to trip you up. It doesn't matter if it is at the workplace, lunch, shopping centers, even sporting events .We are not put here on earth to crawl under a rock and not live. We are put here on purpose. The best thing that can be done is to watch what we intake visually so we won't become sexually stimulated visually. One place to start the guarding of the gates is with television.

TELEVISION

One night I was up late, which for me is between 10:30 and 11:30pm.I was up working on the family budget and needed to unwind. I decided to try to find something funny on television so I could lighten things up for awhile. I started to channel surf for awhile and found a particular comedy show that I had tried to watch before. This particular time the show was totally off base. There was a skit where they showed a man visiting his doctor. The camera panned to the nurse who was so scantily clad she was almost naked. I felt very uncomfortable so I turned off the TV right away. I did not wait for 10 minutes to decide if this was ok or not to watch. After I turned the TV off, I decided to retire for the night and pick up on the budget the next day.

As I ascended upstairs, I was surprised that my wife was still awake. Mona asked me what was I watching on television. I told her what had just happened. She then told me that it is not good for me to watch a show like that, and to maybe consider not watching television late at night. Mona conveyed this to me in such a compassionate way that I totally was in agreement with her. Mona also looked at me in a “firm, yet loving” way that said to me that I better watch myself!!

What's the big deal, you say? The big deal for me was not to let the image of the nurse register and stay with me mentally. This can cause you to concentrate on that other woman; the image that you saw. You will start comparing her to your wife or the young woman you are dating. You will expect your mate to perform, act, and become the images you have focused on!! Trust me-it happens!

It is very subtle. I am an avid sports fan. I am now required to turn the tv channel on some commercials, due to it's content. I don't want or need to see scantily clad women selling me a truck, a mortgage or clothes in a bathing suit.

Movies present the same problem. At least there is a better defense mechanism you can set up with this. Just as with television, you can decide what movie you would like to go and see. You can choose the content by choosing the rating. The only problem is that the R-rated movies are so close to X-rated movies, and the PG-13 films are close to the R-rated films! Choose your cinema wisely!!

There are simple safeguards you can apply to your media viewing(television in particular).Try a couple of these and keep them consistent. Do not beat up on yourself if you drop the ball a couple of times. It is a process, but at the same time get moving on them. They will help you tremendously.

1.Regulate your television time.

Try to avoid late night television. The commercials get very risqué as the night progresses. Sure, watch what you like, but use discretion. Watch out for the commercials. Avoid shows with any sexual content and adult language content. You are probably saying "Sanford, can I watch anything?" Of course you can. You and only you know what triggers you to go and solicit a prostitute or triggers you to look at x rated peep shows. As time goes on you will see how you won't even miss those programs. You will find other things that will occupy that time like writing that business plan you have wanted to do for years. You will discover books that you might have never thought of reading or taking the time to mentor a young man.

2.Be Accountable

If you are married, your wife can be your time keeper. Give her complete access to what you are watching and the authority to ask the tough questions. If you are single and feel tempted by television, have another man call you at a certain time to see if you are ok watching what you are watching. This accountability partner will be a key part in helping overcoming TV viewing habits that are harmful to you.

At all cost protect your fortress. Set boundaries in place for all areas of your life. You would never allow your neighbor to come to your gate and pour garbage into your yard. If your neighbor can't do it, why "dump" the garbage of sexual addiction on yourself?

CHAPTER FOUR
Accountability....True Confessions

"Sanford, I am really glad you took the time to listen to me. I know that I can trust you." My good friend Howard recently echoed those words to me in a recent phone conversation. Howard had just revealed to me some very private information that he had yet to tell his wife. I told Howard that I would not honestly and truthfully tell her this secret. But I did tell Howard that he absolutely must confess to his wife what he had just told me. I was not about to baby sit his dishonesty. With great reluctance, Howard made a true confession to his wife. She was elated to find out that he was man enough to come to her with great transparency. Their relationship has blossomed ever since.

Howard's true confession was based on his relationship with his wife, and his relationship with me. He trusted me. Howard knew I loved and cared enough for him and his wife to stand with him no matter what. He also knew that if HE needed me to, I would "get in his face" and challenge him to always do the proper thing. Howard asked me to be his accountability partner. An accountability partner is someone who you can confide in, particularly about sexual addiction. You will discuss with your accountability partner your victories and your valleys; your inner feelings, and how you can beat sexual addiction.

Accountability is crucial to anyone who is caught up in the seductive addiction of sex. Men are known to be lone rangers and mavericks, especially with this. This fact has sometimes prevented men from developing close, trusting, masculine friendships with each other. Accountability provides the bond with another man to fight all the battles in life. I have mentors and accountability partners for other areas of my life. I really could have benefited by having one in my life during my struggles with this addiction. I now pour into other men with this problem. My accountability partners will ask me in a minute if my television watching has any "seductive overtones"? Maybe they will ask me if I have been in an "uncompromising position" this week with another woman? I have given these men a license to ask as often as they feel led to. They also encourage me when they feel led to ,which is great. Being accountable is a vehicle to freedom from the bondage of sexual addiction. We are not meant to go into battle alone. Look at it as a form of mentorship. Mentors see all the potential you have. It is the same with an accountability partner. This man will keep you from walking into the landmines of life. This type of relationship holds us responsible for the decisions we make. A great thing to know is that YOU ARE GROWING WHEN YOU

SEEK AN ACCOUNTABILITY PARTNER!! You are telling yourself and others in your life that you mean business. The game is over!

When you view pornography or seek the services of a prostitute, there is no one there with you in determining your choices. You have made a conscious decision to go and fall into this trap. Nothing we do goes unaccounted for. We either pay for our choices up front, or pay for them on the back end. Accountability will help us keep out of the trap of sexual addiction.

CHARACTERISTICS OF AN ACCOUNTABILITY PARTNER

Many of you may be saying that this sounds great, but I don't know of anyone that can do this. Maybe there are no men that you know that fit this bill. First, we will look at a few characteristics of an accountability partner. Then, I would like you to re-assess the men in your life and give it a second thought and see who you come up with. I am going to make it very easy for you on the first qualification. A man that is caught up in sexual addiction himself simply can not be an accountability partner. Period. Let's move on.

The ability to encourage is one of the top qualifications for an accountability partner. This should be one of the primary traits you look for. Why? Simple. The absolute last thing you need when battling sexual addiction is someone kicking you emotionally when you are already down. This person needs to understand where you are, where you have been, and how he can encourage you to move in the right direction. Encouragement needs to be based on sincerity. The accountable relationship should be intentional. I have found that men who are genuine and understand the importance of encouragement will help move mountains out of a man's life. You will find these men are great with affirmation as they see you grow step by step away from the darkness of sexual addiction.

Personal space is huge with men. Men are so competitive, secretive, and non-trusting of other men that they shy away from being close to other men. A great accountability partner will recognize that almost immediately. He will sense when to ask the "close questions", and when to be confrontational. When either of these occurs, he will still be there for you afterwards. You may receive a tongue lashing from him time to time, but he has your best interest at heart. If you have a problem with being up close and personal, tell him right off the bat. He will understand and work with you. He is not your enemy, he is your fox hole buddy in this war.

Integrity and honesty must be the calling card of a true accountability partner. He must not think that he is above you at all. His lifestyle must reflect these characteristics. Remember not to associate yourself with someone who has a "bad name". Your accountability partner should not be hot tempered or easily angered. Men can sniff out a phony in a minute. If he says he believes in these character traits but does not exercise them in his daily life, then he is not the accountability partner for you. No matter what he says.

Listening is a lost art form. So many people are caught in "me, me, me", that they simply could care less about what someone is saying to them. I always say to accountability partners that "God gave us two ears and one mouth. So we should listen twice as much and speak less." I personally think that's true. If you ever take the time to listen to someone, they normally will reveal a great deal about themselves. People love to talk about what is going on with them. Listening is crucial to being an accountability partner. Make sure that your partner does this. If he has trouble listening and wants to play "Mr. Fix-It," amicably dissolve the relationship.

Trust is a must. It brings great comfort to you, knowing that what ever part of sexual addiction you are struggling with can be told and kept in confidence. If your accountability partner has been through the fire with this subject, you know you are in a safe relationship. He will understand this is a process. He will not be shocked or dismayed with whatever you may tell him. You will find that no matter what is going on with him, he will take the time to listen to you. Don't be surprised if he acts concerned about other areas of your life. Guess what? He is not acting. He does care about your life and is concerned about YOU. An accountability partner knows that this addiction is based on a root system as we discussed before. To get to the root of any problem, you have got to dig it up. Trust enables you to be "dug up" to plant new soil in your life.

I personally love a good laugh. I will laugh at anything that does not demean a person, country, ethnic group, etc. My golf score is a different story. No, I am not going to tell you my golf score so you can laugh, but, hey, I need to one day break 100!! Have fun and humor in your relationship as well. Keep everything in perspective because this man has been sent to you to help with a serious problem. Respect that and recognize that. But also remember laughter is great medicine for the soul and body.

Loyalty is the one qualification that is significant. It is like being on a team of athletes. Each athlete encourages and spurs each other on. They defend each other. They come together for a common goal and hopefully common good. Your accountability partner will be there at your set time to speak or meet. His conversations will be based on his loyalty to you for he wants nothing more than for you to break free. Respect his loyalty by you being loyal to him as well. Don't keep him in the dark in reference to your addiction to sex.

Please take a few minutes to digest what we have discussed on accountability. Take out a piece of paper and write down the names of at least three men you think of when you hear the word accountability. These men should model integrity, honesty, compassion and leadership qualities in everyday life. They should be loyal, trustworthy, and great encouragers. After you have made the list, set a goal to contact each man within one week. Be honest to these men and explain that you sense and feel sexually tempted often. This is very, very important: MAKE SURE THESE MEN POSSESS THESE CHARACTER TRAITS BEFORE YOU MEET THEM!! The last thing you want is to have someone use what you are telling them against you. Use discretion and your gut instincts as to whom you should meet.

Once this meeting is established and you have "interviewed" your candidates, set up a time and day each week as to when you two men will talk. This meeting can be done via telephone or in person. I strongly recommend that this relationship and meeting does not take place via email. We are talking about establishing a bona fide accountable relationship. Email is just too informal for a bonding such as this.

After you have selected your accountability partner (congratulations!), keep a weekly progress report on yourself. This can be done mentally but I believe in writing things down. Keep a journal of your progress. Write what you are experiencing daily as you daily say no to your flesh. You will be amazed at what will start happening in your life when you start to journal your progress. You will see on paper that by not looking at a woman at work lustfully today, your boss delegated a special project to you that will enhance your career. Get the picture?

You may want to inform your partner that after about three to four weeks, you would like him to give you an assessment or a review of your progress. Let HIM tell you the changes he has seen in you since you are moving away from sexual addiction. Good accountability partners will always tell you the truth, good or bad. He will tell you if you are growing or if you are not stepping up to the plate.

Stay committed to the battle for victory over and beyond sexual addiction. Don't go it alone. Listen, if you need more that one accountability partner, fine. Have two or three if it is needed. Respect their time and take the relationship seriously. A great accountability partner will take you seriously. Even if you can't.

After finding an accountability partner who possesses the character traits in this chapter, I highly recommend a support group. I co-led a support group for men in my church that was open to all faiths and all people. Support groups are another form of accountability. Everything is confidential and some of the most supportive, loving relationships are built through these groups. Support groups are designed to protect you and not comdemn you. ALL INDIVIDUALS ARE WELCOME. Please consult your local directory or the internet to find the closest support group in your area and region.

I have no doubt that one day you will be called on to be an accountability partner. Once you have slain this ugly monster, you will be prepared for good works.

CHAPTER FIVE

Prepare for Good Works

As I drove off the lot of the mission center, I kept saying to myself, " I hope I reached someone tonight." I had just spoken in front of two hundred men in a homeless shelter on a Saturday night. It was summer, a time when most people are thinking of vacation and how many times they are going to the beach this year. My agenda was totally different. I was sent and asked to come to help men see hope.

Six months later I attended a New Years Eve gathering at my mother-in-laws. As the evening began to wind down, I along with my brother-in-law Terry, decided to clean up and take out the garbage. Terry had been in and out of substance abuse and clinics for over twenty years. Interestingly enough, I had been really thinking about him the week leading up to this evening.

As Terry and I walked through the snow covered driveway, I turned to him and said "Terry, I want to talk to you. I just want to tell you a little bit about me. Some of these things you do not know of." Terry turned to me and said, " Oh , I know your story. Do you remember the mission center?" You know, the night you spoke? I was there! I heard every word you said, and I still could not believe you had such an addiction to sex. I didn't think that was even possible."

I don't mean to get real mushy here, but I am man enough to say my eyes were filled with tears. I thanked God for using me as an example to impact another man's life. It was justification for me speaking that night. I speak frequently to groups, particularly to men on this issue. My pain, tears, anger and frustration through my sexual addiction is now helping others get set free. When we go through the fire and come out untouched, people want to know about it.

I had no clue my ordeal with sexual promiscuity would be used to change lives. It was not in my plans at all. I lost so much when I was caught up in the sex web. After having a car repossessed and obtaining mountainous debt, I now know that my sexual exploits were a tool that has turned out for good. After I won the battle and confronted my Goliath, I then became pruned and planted for "good works." Preparation time is never lost time. Being in the crucible solidifies you just like a pure diamond crystal. You come out of the crucible with renewed strength and firmness. You are ready to tell the world, "Look what I lost. I was desperate, broke and yet feeding myself with acts of sex. But, I made it. So can you."

A new mindset comes upon you. Let me go tell someone. Let me help someone. Let's risk going against the grain and culture that pushes self gratification. It takes a man…a real man to stand up for what is right.

Ok, I am not running for political office. But, another man's destiny is tied to your victory. That is absolute truth. Did you know that? YOUR DESTINY IS TIED TO YOUR VICTORY!! Guess what? This book would never have been written if it was not for my addiction to sex AND my recovery. I am now an author, speaker, and accountability partner to others. I am a mentor now. Things are just beginning for me, and you. I can say that because you have reached this part of the book. You now understand how the addiction starts, some of the root causes of sexual addiction, and a road map to victory. You did not talk the talk, you are walking the walk.

I have learned that our lives are not for us to live "comfortably." Comfortable lives can bring grave consequences. We start to tell ourselves that we are invincible and we can do everything alone. Nothing can be farther from the truth. If you think that you can be alone at a bar or lounge with a woman and not feel tempted to say or do something, you are fooling yourself. I have been free from sexual addiction for years and would not consider this. You need help to get set free so you can go and help someone. There are people that I will not be able to reach, but you will reach them with ease. I can name numerous athletes, politicians, entertainers, cooks, mechanics, you name it that would love to hear your story. It would save them public scrutiny and embarrassment. Not to mention time and money.

So my question to you is are you ready and prepared for good works? Will you fight FOR your family, your health, your finances, YOUR FUTURE? Well, I am going to operate on the premise that you are ready to get into battle. Let's suit up and let's go!!

THE BATTLE PLAN

You now have more than enough weapons in your arsenal. If you are going to claim victory, you must know where the enemy lies and strategically attack. Once you have taken enemy territory, you will be awarded with abundance in the following areas.

Closer Family	Job Promotions
Better Health	Ministry
Exciting Marriage	Career Advancement
Financial Breakthroughs	Business Deals
Sense Of Purpose	Peace

These are just a few things that are laid up in the enemies camp. Every man has a treasure chest with these in it. Some have fought for these and have not attained them yet due to sexual addiction. Some men are not blessed with these things because it just may lead them down the road of sexual addiction. Great coaches and leaders have a game plan. The plan for you is for the next 21 days to concentrate on stopping one sexual addictive act per day. If you look at three porno movies a day, you are going to do every thing to abstain from it. If it is a certain time that you do it, find something else to substitute for it. You may have to go for a ride, read, or better yet, get out a pad and write what you are feeling. Remember it is a process. The idea is to reduce and eliminate your sexually addictive acts DAILY. This includes phone sex, pornography(all forms),adultery, massage parlors, prostitution, movies and sexually suggestive television. These are just a few examples, but changing directions is what we are trying to do here.

Every day at the end of the day write down what happened when you gave up your addiction for the day. After 21 days you will see some amazing results, but YOU MUST STICK IT OUT. That is the key.

CONCLUSION

If I could some up everything in one word I would. I simply can not. I would like to thank the men and women who have purchased this book. I hope that you have laughed a little during the journey, and I hope the book encourages you as well. You have a bright future and have yet to arrive. Expect victory. Once this issue of sexual addiction has been confronted, get ready to live life at a brand new level!!

ACKNOWLEDGEMENTS

I would first of all like to thank God who showed me a gift I had that I was unaware of. Without HIM, there is no me. My sister Rhonda Ashley and brother Cedric Ashley, who are both always good for a great time no matter what is going on in their lives! Pastor Ron Gonzalez for being the first one ever to give me a shot at writing, and knowing me better than many others. Thanks Dr. David Ireland for "hearing from God" one Sunday morning and speaking to me about writing. Your humble heart is beyond words. Pastor Anthony Franklin for letting me open my heart to many through men's ministry. Thanks to all my mentors who have encouraged me over the years and who continuously pour into me today. Very special thanks to Wes Hall for loving me and showing me how to always believe and think big!! Thank you Pastor Frank Al Dunkins for ALWAYS being there!!

THANK YOU ALL!!!!!

For Further Information Contact Sanford Ashley at…...

<u>www.sanfordashley.com</u>

or

sanfordashley@comcast.net

About The Author

Sanford Ashley is a writer, speaker, and business executive. He addresses many issues that are pertinent to succeeding in life. He has a special gift for impacting and changing men's lives. Sanford has been published in national magazines such as Sales and Marketing Management Magazine, Men of Integrity (Promise Keepers) and Gospel Today. Sanford co-led a support group for those who struggle with sexual addiction at Christ Church in Montclair, N.J. He speaks frequently at companies, men's groups, retreats and teaches on how to have a successful small group for men. Sanford resides in New Jersey with his adoring wife Mona, and sons Malachi and Brandon.